RECLAIM YOUR POWER!

RECLAIM

YOUR

POWER!

A 30–Day Guide to Hope, Healing, and
Inspiration for Men of Color

TERRANCE DEAN

VILLARD / NEW YORK

Library of Congress Cataloging-in-Publication Data

Dean, Terrance.
Reclaim your power!: a 30-day guide to hope, healing, and inspiration
for men of color / by Terrance Dean.
p.   cm.
Includes bibliographical references.
ISBN 978-0-8129-6778-4 (trade paper)
1. African American men—Life skills guides.   2. African American men—
Conduct of life.   3. African American men—Religious life.   4. Power
(Philosophy).   5. Hope.   6. Mental healing.   7. Inspiration.   I. Title

E185.86 .D397 2003   158.1'089'96073—dc21   2002034346

Villard Books website: www.villard.com

Book design by JoAnne Metsch

146470499

THANK YOU, FATHER, for your many blessings you have bestowed upon my life. Thank you for allowing me to be a vessel for your work and service. To God be the glory.

This book is dedicated to my grandmother, Pearl Williams, my mother, Blanche Gerald, and my brothers, George Gerald and Jevonte Gerald. Their spirits soar in the heavens, and they continue to be my guardian angels. To my sister, Sheritta Gerald, who knows her big brother loves her and to my amazing nephew, Mitchell. To my aunts, uncles, and cousins who continue to be the greatest supporting family anyone can dream of having. This book is also dedicated to many wonderful friends who have been of great assistance in my journey. Last, to all the men of Men's Empowerment, Inc.—you all are true examples of what greatness, grace, power, and love look like.

FOREWORD

Not long ago, I made the profound realization that my community desperately needs access to power. More specifically, my community—and all communities, for that matter—need to discover resources that will enlighten, inspire, and transform our lives for the better. What kind of wisdom am I talking about? What kind of knowledge could this be? Fortunately, the answer is right in front of our eyes.

For me, this easily accessible power is rooted in the reality that communities are fashioned by *choice*. Every day, and every moment, we make choices about what kind of people we want to be and what kind of communities we want to sustain. With this thinking, black people are free to choose whether to live in stably designed communities—by choice—or needlessly subsist in unwarranted barracks of discontent.

Armed with this "wisdom," a new generation of leaders is beginning to ponder alternatives. Men and women are slowly starting to accept the reality that we now possess the collaborative means to bring an end to our collective suffering. Each day more converted statesmen and citizens are lining up to challenge every form and face of oppression. Whether it is deciding to tackle drugs, homelessness, self-hatred, or despair, more and more people are accepting the responsibility of progressive social service. As a result, I now believe, more than ever, that we are starting to see the first fruits of the cultural renaissance that is going to resurrect our pride and politics.

Moreover, I also believe, and I urge more of you to join me in this thinking, that a chosen generation is being pruned, that ancient wounds are beginning to heal, and that despite every indication to the contrary, we collectively recognize the answer to the so-called Negro problem. All we need to do is survey our options, make the right choices, and behold our power. It is for this reason that this book is so important.

It is now time for black men to step up. As many of you have read, more and more experts are realizing that the pivotal role men play in the stability of family and community is far more profound than previously thought. Not only do we have the power to build and fortify, we also have the ability, by our absence, to equally deter and destroy. Therefore, as we consider the next stage of our sojourn in America, it is imperative that every brother plays his part. And what is this part? What role are we supposed to play? At this juncture, I think we simply need men who will choose to be fathers. And I don't mean making the choice because it's fun, or convenient, or even easy, but simply because it's our responsibility. I think we have seen enough of the "baby daddy" syndrome. At this moment, our babies need fathers, and our wives and mothers need husbands. Even if you disagree with me, I think this revival alone will change the world. In another sense, I also think our generation needs more men who will simply *branch out on their own*. Whether it is starting a new business, starting a prayer group, or starting a charter school, we need men who will survey the landscape and also dream a world. As Scripture points out, "Without vision, the people will die."

Lastly, and these points shouldn't even need to be mentioned, we need brothers who will regularly vote with conscience, generously provide care for our elders, and aggressively preserve our dignity by responding to the avalanche of injustice that subsists in our environments in the form of gangs, violence, and crime. These victories alone are revolutionary and will help us walk safely in our own neighborhoods and live increasingly without fear. And that is precisely what this book is about: responding to the call as we learn from each other, enlighten one another, and step up without fear.

In my recent book, *Keeping the Faith*, I endeavored to uncover the collective wisdom of our community at large. In this book, I hope you will discover the counsel of other black men who have specific words and wisdom for all of us. For me, this was especially gratifying work because very seldom do we find books that are intentionally designed for our growth and edification as black men. Unfortunately, even though a lot of work still needs to be done in this regard, too many of us, it seems, are failing to make this inward journey a priority. But the choice is yours. And the time is now.

Over the years, my personal call has been advocating for the increased empowerment of the African-American community. While this labor has certainly involved raising my own voice, it has also involved the necessity of bringing other voices into the chorus. As you read these pages, I hope that you will enjoy these new visionaries and discover a fresh melody to insert into your library, your consciousness, and into the very movement itself. And regardless of your opinion of philosophy, let us always remember that no matter what the media may tell us, black people are forever linked in a common course of destiny, and that we are our brothers' keepers.

Together in Spirit.

TAVIS SMILEY, author, and host of *The Tavis Smiley Show*, NPR
October 8, 2002
Los Angeles, CA

CONTENTS

INTRODUCTION

REMEMBER WALKING to work at MTV Networks from the train station. I heard a big booming voice asking, "What are you doing?"

It startled me at first because I had heard the voice before. Spirit was speaking, and it was serious because it was a booming voice, not subtle as I had perceived it before. I replied to Spirit, "What do you mean, what am I doing?" At this point, tears started to flood my eyes. I knew I had been running from what Spirit was guiding me to do. That was in the year 2000.

I am used to the voice of Spirit because I had been hearing it since I was a child. I remember Spirit speaking to me when my aunt took me to church every Sunday. It was there that I had found my solitude and time to talk directly with God about what was happening and going on in my life. I had learned how to be still, to listen and be obedient to the voice of Spirit.

I went away to college in Nashville, because I wanted to get away from my family. I wanted to escape my past of pain, hurt, anger, and bitterness. After graduation from college, I just ran, ran, and ran. I got so far from home that I had little to no contact with anyone from my family. I did this on purpose because I was angry with my family—I literally despised my mother.

My mother was a heroin addict. She used drugs heavily. Everyone in the family knew of her addiction, yet no one stepped in to help her seek professional help. We just learned to deal with it. My mother's heavy drug use resulted in her becoming a prostitute to support her drug habit.

Imagine being a young boy growing up seeing your mother being dropped off by various men in different cars. Imagine watching your mother going into the bathroom and not coming out for two or three hours, obviously high on some drug. Imagine being in a car with your friends and driving out of the way to avoid certain neighborhoods and streets because you were afraid they would see your mother on the corner picking up "johns" for a trick.

I was so upset and angry that I was not born to what I considered a "normal" family. I was bitter because all my friends appeared to have normal families, with mothers who took them to the park, took them out to dinner, or attended their high school or college graduations.

I went to college because I swore I would not let my life end up like so many others I had known. I definitely did not want to end up like my mother. I fought like hell to buck the system to work in my favor. I worked hard in school and, just when I thought all was well, I got the call that my mother was sick. She had developed the AIDS virus from sharing drug needles.

When I got this call, I was shocked and startled. It had such a grip on me. I knew I was going to lose my mother. As it was close to Christmas break from school, I decided to go home immediately once the break started.

I went home and spent many days with my mother. We talked so much that it was actually refreshing to let my guard of anger and bitterness down. As the trip came to an end, I packed my bags and began preparations for my return to school.

As I was leaving and walking out the door, my mother called to me. I stopped at the door, turned to hear her voice and, for the first time in my life, my mother gently said, "I love you." I replied back, "I love you, too," and walked out the door, crying uncontrollably. I knew it would be the last time I would see her alive.

I was able to return to school and graduate because I knew that was what my mother would have wanted. After graduation I got an internship with CNN in Washington, D.C.; I did not want to return home to Detroit because I was still angry with my family for not helping my mother and constantly shuffling my sister and brothers, who were younger, from family to family.

As I continued to run from my family to avoid my pain and hurt, I got yet another call. My two younger brothers had also developed the AIDS virus, which eventually would claim their lives as well. My youngest brother, Jevonte, who had been infected with the disease while still in my mother's womb, died two years after my mother's death. He was three years old. My other brother, George, who was infected while he was molested in a group home for young boys, was nineteen years old when he died.

My life seemed to have turned upside down. I couldn't deal with any more death and pain, so I continued to delve into work and traveled as frequently as possible. I had to keep moving and doing something to keep my mind active, so I wouldn't think of what was happening in my family.

Then, in the year 2000, I heard the voice of Spirit, asking if I was ready to stop running and start healing. Spirit said, "I have work for you to do, and you need some healing."

I had no other choice but to be obedient to Spirit. For the first time, I sat alone and cried. I cried for all the pain I had endured. I cried for all the years I had lost with my family. I cried because I had lost my mother and two brothers. I cried because I was tired of running, and I needed rest.

Spirit immediately went to work, and I began the healing. I began my spiritual work with mentors and healers, who literally showed up when I surrendered and helped me access my power and rebuild my spiritual muscle. I needed to be strong for the work I was about to embark upon.

I am glad I was able to surrender and let love move in. I am glad I was able to forgive everyone around me. Even more important, I'm glad I was able to forgive myself.

Once Spirit started working, I created the organization Men's Empowerment, Inc. I knew there were other men dealing with situations and conditions similar to my own. I wanted to create a place where men could come and share their pains, joys, and difficulties, a place where they could tell their stories.

In creating Men's Empowerment, I had no idea it would grow as rapidly as it did. Within four years, the organization has grown from 20 to more than 250 men of color, all of whom responded in the affirmative that they were looking for an outlet to express their emotions and a place where they could go for healing. It is a great feeling to walk into a room with brothers from various backgrounds coming together for one common cause: to nurture their spirits for healing.

The product of my surrendering and healing is this book, which I share with other men who are seeking to surrender and heal their lives. I have learned so much that I know it is time to share with my fellow brothers. It's now time that we let one another know it's okay to cry and let down our guards. It's okay to feel pain and surrender to love when it shows up. It's okay to talk with another brother about what's going on in your life. We need this dialogue more than ever in our lives.

In creating this book, I wanted to share with other men of color the joys, pains, frustrations, and love I have had the opportunity to be a part of. I have found that our sisters, mothers, aunts, and mates have created their own support systems and foundations to help nurture one another in spirit. They have created so many outlets to sustain their inner selves that it is only a natural progression for men to get it and catch up.

More of us are starting and creating our own support systems and groups. Even if we have only one buddy to share with, we are creating a space for ourselves to share and open up, to allow Spirit room to move and grow. As men, we generally don't allow others to witness or experience this space within us.

This book was inspired by all the men with whom I have had the opportunity to share experiences both joyful and painful, experiences that have led me to an amazing journey with Spirit. In this journey, I have discovered some amazing things about myself. I have learned that I am fearless, worthy, valuable, and, more important, I am love. I choose love daily and in all my interactions. I choose love because love has chosen me.

While you are reading this book, be sure to perform the daily activities. They will be extremely helpful to your development throughout the month. Make sure to practice the day's inspiration, and witness the results of your behavior. Use the exercise pages to write down your experiences, how you actually feel when you incorporate the inspirations into your life. I know that when I was able to write down what was happening in my life, it was much easier to work through, because I had gotten the information out of my head and put it down on paper in front of me. I was then able to see the dialogue going on in my head and the drama that was ruling my life.

It's no accident that you have this book in your hands. You or someone you know has thought enough about you to get you started or help you remember your connection to Spirit. Know that everything is divinely created and that you are meant to be here, right now, at this time, to become aware of your greatness. I encourage you to read this book and be open to its message.

I share this book with all my fellow brothers, uncles, fathers, and grandfathers. I share this book with my ancestors, who came before me and created a path for me to be a voice and a beacon of light unto the world. I share this book with family, who so graciously loved and nurtured me. I share this book with my grandmother, mother, and brothers, who have passed on to become my spiritual guides. Finally, I share this book with all the sisters, aunts, mothers, and grandmothers who continue to love all men.

RECLAIM YOUR POWER!

DAY 1

Listen

The friends who listen to us are the ones we move toward.

—ADEYEMI BANDELE,
executive director, Men on the Move

s WE WORK to further our careers, deal with family, or hang with friends, we often seem to be talking, yelling, or screaming. As men, we want to appear as if we can take charge and command an audience. We are so caught up in having people hear us that we do not take the time to listen; and thus we often miss the message or lesson that is being taught.

God speaks to us ever so gently. Listening involves being quiet, being able to still yourself to hear the voice of Spirit. The message may come from a song, e-mail, book, friend, family member, or co-worker. In order to hear, however, you will have to learn to listen.

Start today by agreeing to listen to Spirit. You can create a private "listening" space somewhere in your office or home. Close your office door for five minutes. Step outside the office building. Find solitude in your basement or your bedroom. Find a space where you can be alone. You will be amazed at the clarity you will have when you are able to allow Spirit to speak, while you simply listen.

Make a list of the times when

Spirit was guiding you, but you

avoided it by not listening.

How will you incorporate

listening into your life today?

DAY

2

Be Still

There is a soul force in the universe, which, if we permit it, will flow through us and produce miraculous results.

— MAHATMA GANDHI

E RUSH TO get to the next thing—a meeting, the recording studio, or the office. We are always running, "being busy making moves." Even when we are not required to be somewhere, we find something to keep us busy. As men, we seem to think that if we are not hustling and bustling, then we are missing out on something.

To be still simply requires us not to do anything. To stop: stop moving, stop running, and stop creating things to do when we feel bored.

Spirit may be trying to guide us one way, but we move in another. Spirit may want us to simply be and enjoy the moment. When we take the time to be still, we allow Spirit to move into our lives.

Today, before you run to your next meeting, dash to the studio, or start a new project, allow yourself to be still. Relax and settle yourself in a quiet place somewhere in your office or home.

Enjoy the moment and let yourself be led in the direction of love, peace, and harmony.

List the things that prevent you

from being still. How can

you start being still today?

DAY

3

Show Kindness

Do not speak harshly to anyone; those who are spoken to will answer thee in the same way. Angry speech is painful: Blows for blows will touch thee.

— BUDDHA,
The Dhammapada (c. 300 B.C.)

E ARE SOMETIMES called upon to work long hours, go the extra mile, or clean up the mess when everyone's gone. But along the way, we tend to forget to show kindness to those around us, be they family, friends, co-workers, or especially strangers.

As men, we may feel that if we show kindness others will view us as weak or vulnerable. We expect people to excuse our rude or harsh behavior because we're men.

To show kindness allows life to bring kindness to us. When we are able to be compassionate or to say thank you for a job well done, we are allowing Spirit to be free to express itself.

Today, show kindness to someone. Tell a co-worker what a great job he or she is doing. Tell the intern in your department that you appreciate his or her help. Let your friends know you appreciate them for taking your late-night calls when you need to talk. Compliment your mate, and let her know how much you appreciate her. Tell your kids how proud you are of them in spite of your expectations of them. Remember, your children are learning life just as you once did, so be patient and loving with them.

When you show kindness, the anger and bitterness inside of you subsides. Random acts of kindness will, in fact, allow you to be seen as a compassionate and strong man.

Make a list of people who can

benefit from your kindness. To

whom will you show kindness today?

DAY

4

Be Obedient to Guidance from Spirit

If there is something you know you should be doing but don't feel like doing it . . . do it anyway!

— NATHAN SCOTT,
actor

D O YOU EVER have the urge to speak to someone you do not know? Have you ever suddenly wanted to share a kind word, hold a hand, or give someone a hug? Have you ever felt you should walk or drive in a different direction? Has something told you to pick up a certain book or listen to a certain song? These actions are Spirit guiding you.

As men, we are always getting in the way of Spirit with our manner of thinking. We feel we know what's best for us, and we begin to out-think ourselves. When we receive these divine interventions to do or say something, we feel we can't share what we've been given to do because we are fearful of the response we will receive.

When we are obedient to guidance from Spirit, we are actually allowing ourselves to be a vessel of healing or blessing to ourselves and to others.

Today, be obedient to guidance from Spirit. Get out of the way, and let Spirit move and work. Give in to the fear, and allow the love to flow from you to others. It does not serve you to hold on to the feeling that Spirit wishes you to share with others. It is frustrating to hold on to something so precious; therefore, next time you get that sudden urge, go with it, and be with it.

EXERCISE

Make a list of the ways you have been

ignoring guidance from Spirit.

What will you do now to be

obedient to guidance from Spirit?

DAY

5

Trust Yourself

Truth is more than a mental exercise.

— THURGOOD MARSHALL,
first black justice of the U.S. Supreme Court

HINK ABOUT THIS: Has there ever been a moment when you've felt that you've had nothing or no one else to rely upon but yourself? Has there ever been a moment when you've known that you only had your own judgment to depend upon?

Some of us have friends and family members who question our decisions. They wonder if our careers are right for us, or they offer advice about our relationships, saying, "You don't belong in that relationship" or "He or she is no good for you." Our family and friends have good intentions; however, only we are responsible for our lives, and only we can trust ourselves to know that we are doing what's right for us at any particular moment.

The only person who knows the truth of your being is *you*. The only person who can responsibly know what is best for you is *you*. That is why it is important to learn to trust yourself in spite of your fears and what others think you should be doing.

When you are in tune with your Spirit, and you speak from the truth of your Spirit, you learn to trust yourself. You no longer doubt yourself or act from fear. There are times when you are not right; these are opportunities to trust yourself to be honest with those around you. These are the times to be led to a space of pure love. When you act from love, the truest essence of your Spirit, you trust yourself to be led to guidance.

In trusting yourself, you stand affirmed in your choice and let what is, simply *be*. When you trust yourself, you begin to see yourself as courageous and brave, despite what your mind may be telling you. In operating with Spirit, you simply know you are within the divine working of what is so.

Today, trust yourself. You'll be surprised to see yourself smile in the face of fear.

Write down some of the times

when you have not trusted yourself.

How are you going to start

trusting yourself?

Be Unpredictable and Spontaneous

The main point in the game of life is to have fun. We are afraid to have fun because somehow that makes life too easy.

— SAMMY DAVIS, JR.,
entertainer

O YOU TAKE THE same route to work each morning? Do your loved ones know what you're going to say or do before *you* do? Do you have the same daily routine? Today, look at your everyday habits. It's amazing how we unconsciously do the same things in our lives, over and over again.

We become so predictable that we stop allowing ourselves to do anything new or exciting. It's easy to do the things we've grown accustomed to or become comfortable with. But when we do this, we are preventing Spirit from helping us experience the fullness of life.

Today, choose to be unpredictable and spontaneous. Call a loved one and plan a special evening out. Take a different route to work. Change the time you go to lunch, choose a different restaurant, and try eating something different. Pick up a book by an author whom you've never read before. Watch as a whole new realm of possibilities opens up to you.

EXERCISE

List all the things that you

have always thought of doing.

Now write the ways you can

be unpredictable and spontaneous

in your life.

D A Y

7

Be Responsible

There are no secrets to success: don't waste time looking for them. Success is the result of perfection, hard work, and learning from failure.

—COLIN POWELL,
Secretary of State

E BLAME EVERYONE for the state of our lives. We blame "the man" for not giving us a job. We blame the father who was not a part of our life. We blame our loved ones for not showing us enough love or care. We blame the school system for the lack of teachers and their inability to teach us. And we blame society for everything that is happening to us.

When are we going to start taking responsibility for ourselves? It is easy to blame someone else for what happens, but it is not going to solve the problem or create a new opportunity. We dwell on what happened to us, and thus create a life story for this event so we can have something to complain about.

Today, be responsible. Take charge of your life, and do not blame anyone else for what happened to you. You have more control than you think. Be responsible for your educational experience. Get your diploma or degree. Go to the library or bookstore, and get books that will increase your knowledge.

Be responsible for your career. Update your resume. Find out about free resume-writing services or job-coaching seminars. Be responsible in your job search. Set up an informational interview with a company you are interested in working for. Find out who is in the position you would like to have and meet with that person.

Be responsible with your family. Love them, and allow them to love you. Go to dinner with your loved one. Attend your child's recital or game.

To be responsible for your life is to be responsible for what you want life to give you.

In what ways have you not

been responsible with your life?

What can you do now to

take responsibility for your life?

DAY

8

Do Your Best

As simple as it sounds, when I was growing up my father often impressed upon me to simply "do my best" in whatever endeavor was before me. But I also like the way Lenny Kravitz put it when he penned the lyric "It ain't over 'til it's over"—I've been known to spend days perfecting a lyric, and through God's grace, it has paid off. I've learned that the details do matter.

—GORDON CHAMBERS,
Grammy Award–winning lyricist

L IFE SHOWS UP to us as we show up to it: We can't half-step or be late. We must give our full effort and play the whole game. We can't be ready to bail out when things don't go our way.

We just have to do our best.

When you allow Spirit to come through in your life, it will help you find ways to do your best, to be the best in your career, with your family, and with your friends. The light in *you* will shine so brightly that life will not have any other choice but to provide the most for you.

If you want life to give you what you deserve, then you have to earn it.

You can always increase your game. When you are given opportunities to shine, go the extra mile. When your boss gives you an assignment, add an extra creative edge. When your loved one asks for a minute of your time, give him or her an hour, and give your undivided attention.

Today, do your best and the best will come to you.

EXERCISE

Have you been doing your best?

How can you start?

D A Y

9

Can't No One Stop You but You

The greatest strength is within; you are born with unlimited potential. Know thyself and know God. Maximize your greatest power, identify with the Spirit and never, ever be satisfied.

— MAXIE C. JACKSON III,
general manager, WEAA 88.9 FM, Morgan
State University National Public Radio,
Baltimore, Maryland

EN ARE DETERMINED to win no matter what. We are creatures who love to conquer. When we see something we want, we do everything in our power to get it—except save our communities and ourselves.

How many times have you told yourself that you were not good enough to do something? How many times have you told yourself that you were not smart enough to get that job, move upward in your career, or go back to school?

We prevent ourselves from winning. We create our own obstacles. No one has put hurdles in our way, or set us up to fail. We create our own hurdles and failures. We believe we cannot do something, so we give up. We give up in our jobs because we feel the color of our skin won't allow us to be promoted. We give up in our communities because we feel the youth won't listen to us. As men we have many responsibilities to our families, which include making decisions for the household and preserving the well-being of our mates and children. We have to rely upon our paternal instincts to know our children are well while at the same time being mindful of the morals and values we put upon them. There are some men who have to care for their elderly parents, assist with other family members' children, and still be a brother, uncle, and friend to those in need. These pressures can appear to be insurmountable. We have so many things on our plates and little time to juggle them all. And sometimes we give up on ourselves because we believe we can't be *who* we want or have *what* we want.

Can't no one stop you but you. If you want to move upward in your career and your boss won't promote you, ask to speak with him or her about your performance. Get an evaluation of what you need to improve on and areas in which you can be better. If this does not work, there are other companies that will hire someone with your talent. Can't no one stop you but you.

Whatever you so desire or want in life, you can have. Spirit is unlimited—so why do you put limits on *your* life?

Today, tell yourself, "Can't no one stop me but me."

What are some

of the challenges and obstacles you are

currently facing? What can you

start doing today to overcome

these challenges?

Be a Part of Your Community

Never exalt people because they're in your family; never exalt people because they're your color; never exalt people because they're your kinfolk. Exalt them because they're worthy.

— THE HONORABLE MINISTER LOUIS
FARRAKHAN,
leader of the Nation of Islam

OW MANY TIMES have you walked through your community without supporting the local businesses? How many times have you bypassed the children in the neighborhood because you were too busy to be bothered? Some of us barely know our neighbors or even the person who lives next door to us. We are so consumed with our own lives that we don't realize that *we* are our community.

We are the kings of our communities. We are the future of our children. If we do not support and lead our communities, we don't allow ourselves to grow and to be our brothers' keepers.

Spirit is about communal experience. It is about sharing yourself with others. When you become a part of your community, you allow Spirit the opportunity to experience sharing with others outside your immediate circle.

To be a part of your community means you must open up to your community. Next time you are walking in your community, stop in on a local vendor or business owner. Get to know the services they offer. Find out what organizations or outreach programs exist for children or adults. Your talents and experiences may lend themselves to being a teacher or specialist to someone else. You never know the life you may be able to assist.

Today, find out how you can be a part of your community.

List some of the problems

and challenges of your community.

What can you do about them

to improve your community?

Be a Mentor

No matter how high you soar, never lose sight of
the ground.

— DERRICK THOMPSON,
entertainment executive

E ARE OUR brothers' keepers. We have developed skills, gained knowledge, and obtained wisdom along our paths. We have made choices that were beneficial for our careers, and we have made choices that we wish not to repeat.

Someone you know is living their life just as you did. An intern in your department is looking to make a career in the field you have mastered. There is someone in your community people have labeled "bad" or a youth who needs guidance.

Be a mentor. You are the best teacher to that child, intern, or colleague. You have been in the same situation, you know what the outcome will be from certain decisions, and you are aware of life's lessons. Your Spirit wants to share these experiences with others.

What serves us best is giving of ourselves, giving of our time to assist someone along the way. To be a mentor, you allow access to yourself so others can learn and be part of your life.

Today, start being a mentor. If you know of someone who needs guidance or assistance, be a mentor to them. The mentor you are to them, the mentor life is to you.

Have you had mentors in your life?

If so, who?

If you have not been a mentor,

who could you mentor?

DAY 12

Forgiveness

Forgive, and you will be forgiven.

— LUKE 6:37

HERE HAVE BEEN times when people have crossed you, made you upset, or did something wrong to you. You vowed to get revenge or not to let their mistreatment of you go by unnoticed. Every time you see that person or hear about the incident it makes you flare up and become angry all over again. You have made it a point not to forget what has been done to you.

Forgiveness is the key to our hearts. It is the passport to love and peace. Holding on to anger and bitterness toward someone you feel may have done you wrong is not going to make the situation or your relationship any better. Do you realize that holding on to anger and bitterness toward someone actually allows that person or situation to have power over you?

When you are unable to forgive, how do you expect others to forgive you when you have done something to them? We sometimes forget how we make others upset or cause pain in another person's life. We even think it's ridiculous that they won't forgive us for something that may appear to be small or blown way out of proportion.

Just think about the times you have done the same to another. They feel and think the same way as you do when others don't forgive you.

Forgiving is a huge healing factor in our lives. It allows us to supercede our humanness and be of our true spiritual essence. Forgiving requires power and the courage to know that we are all human and we all make mistakes. You realize that giving your power over to anger is not going to move you forward but hinder you.

Forgive yourself and forgive others. Forgive yourself first and foremost. When you forgive yourself, you get to see your humanness. Don't beat up on yourself because you failed to do something or you didn't meet your expectations when you planned to. Everything has a due season and time.

Today, take the time to forgive. You will heal yourself and your relationships. When you forgive, you will be forgiven.

EXERCISE

Make a list of people you would

like to forgive or create a

new relationship with.

(Put yourself first.)

DAY

13

Show Emotion

I am so blessed. Thank you, God, for everything that you have given me. Please help me to be strong and positive . . . and not buy into evil, negativity, or hate. Forgive me and help me to forgive. Help me to be kind, loving, and compassionate.

— EMIL WILBEKIN,
cultural ambassador

E MEN ARE probably the only creatures afraid to show emotion. We believe that we will be seen as weak, that people will not take us seriously if we show emotion. We feel that if we were to break down and cry or tell our mates how much we love them it will somehow leave us vulnerable. Even when we are asked how we are doing, our initial response is usually, "I'm fine." This mechanical response is only a cover-up for our fear of actually telling someone, "I'm not having a good day," or "I've been through a lot lately, so I need someone to listen," or "I've been blessed beyond measure and God is truly working in my life."

But by not showing certain emotions we invalidate our Spirit. We cause pain and discomfort in our lives. We try to hold our emotions in to avoid embarrassment or the feelings associated with experiencing emotion.

However, we are quick to show our anger and disgust. We let these negative emotions define ourselves. We are mad at everything and everyone around us. We are too afraid to show our joy and sadness and, more important, we are too afraid to show our love.

Love is who we are; we are *of love*. It is difficult not to express what we are created from. To show emotion is not going to do any harm or damage to us; rather it will free us from fear and disease. In some cases, not showing emotion but suppressing it can cause heart disease, stress, and high blood pressure.

Release the emotions you feel. If you are sad, express your sadness. If you are joyous, express your joy. If you want to cry, cry. It will save your life. More important, show love. Be of love in all you do. Know that Spirit is really trying to express its love in all experiences.

So today, whatever you are feeling, show it and let yourself and others see your humanity.

Make a list of the circumstances

past and present that have caused

you to show your emotions.

Acknowledge the emotions

you are suppressing and

wish to release.

Faith

While spectators watch you come in first, they don't get to see your true starting point. Winning is not what others think of you, but what you think of yourself. Start your day knowing that victory is always yours!

—THE HONORABLE WILLIAM A. ALLEN,
New York State Assembly district leader
(70th district, Harlem, New York)

TO HAVE FAITH is to know that whatever you desire or ask for will be granted unto you, that whatever the situation or problem, your faith will see you through. You only need to have faith the size of a mustard seed.

We deal with so many things in life on a daily basis. We have to solve problems, answer questions, fix this, and make that happen. In some instances, we are not sure what we are doing, what steps to take, or if it will all work out. In these moments, we have to lean not on our own understanding, but simply rely on faith.

Faith moves mountains. Faith is to know that it *will* be done. Faith is not doubt or fear, but true belief when we say, "And so it is."

Whenever you are uncertain about what to do in a situation or anxious about what life has in store for you, know that Spirit is operating in faith, that all questions are answered, and whatever you ask is given unto you. Now sometimes we may not like the answers or the product of what we asked for and we tend to say that God is not listening or has not answered our request. We tend to think in our terms of time when we make our request, so when it does not appear at the appropriate time we think our request must not be in accordance to Spirit; however, because we don't speak in specifics with Spirit, then what we ask may be answered or provided for us in a day, a month, a year, or several years. That is why a wise man only speaks when necessary; fools speak unknowingly and forget what they speak.

Today, have faith.

What experience has made

you uncertain or doubtful?

Are you willing to release

it and have faith?

D A Y

15

Have Integrity

The spirit indeed is willing, but the flesh is weak.

— MATTHEW 26:41

OMETIMES WE SAY things we don't mean, or to which we know we are not committed. We make plans and appointments, and we show up late, or we don't show up at all. We don't have integrity with our families, friends, communities, or ourselves. We don't keep our word because doing so would require us to be responsible.

Responsibility requires us to show integrity for who we are, and having integrity is about being true to your word. Your word is who you are. It is all you have. When you claim to be who you are, people listen.

As men, we must commit to having integrity. We say that we will be on time, pay the bills, make the arrangements, or keep our appointments. We need to do what we say we are going to do. We must keep our word, and show up when we say we are going to show up. Sometimes events happen in our lives, and we are not able to keep our commitments. These times are exceptions. Have integrity when you plan or when you enter into agreements.

Your life cannot be about making excuses for your behavior. Be a man of your word. That is all people have to know of you. Be who you say you are.

Today, have integrity, and you will feel powerful when you show up on time to your appointments, job, family, and your life.

Make a list of people or situations

to which you made a commitment,

yet did not keep your word.

How can you have more

integrity in your life?

DAY

16

Move, Mountain, Get out of My Way!

Fall down seven times, stand up eight.

— STACY SPIKES,
CEO, Urbanworld Film Group

IFE IS HAPPENING every second, and with it comes problems, situations, issues, and anything else we can imagine. We encounter these bumps in the road and immediately decide we can't handle the situation. We see life coming at us and we dodge, leap, cover, and run from it. Life is going to happen, regardless of how much we want to get out of its way.

We have to be relentless with ourselves to deal with our family, friends, co-workers, and community. We have to demand *more* of ourselves. It is easy to remain complacent, to adhere to the comforts of life and to what we are willing to give.

When you feel as if you can't do any more, push for more. When you feel it won't be worth it, make it worthwhile. Yes, you've given it all you are willing to give, but have you given it all you can? Sometimes we have to stand up and say, "Move, mountain, get out of my way!" You never know the possibilities that will open up when you commit yourself to your life.

Today, move those mountains, and get them out of your way.

What mountains are you ready

to move out of your way?

Enjoy the Journey

The past is a ghost, the future a dream and all we ever have is now.

— BILL COSBY,
entertainer, humanitarian

O YOU REMEMBER the day you graduated from high school? The day you met your first love? Do you even remember the day you learned to ride a bike? Remembering these times allows you to enjoy the journey.

Some amazing things happen in life. The seasons change, a child is born, or you fall in love for the first time. Yet in our lives, we are busy going here and going there. We get so caught up in moving through life that we never get to enjoy the event or the occasion. It is your life. Enjoy the journey.

Think about the times you've said to yourself, "That was fun; I wish I had more time to enjoy it" or "I wish this moment could last forever." Those moments happened, and you can only relive them in memory.

Issues and problems are only momentary. Life is forever, and your time here is not guaranteed. Don't worry about tomorrow, for you do not know what tomorrow holds. Don't worry about the past; it happened. You can change how you will act and be *now*. Enjoy the journey.

There are mountains to be climbed, trails to be blazed, cities to be seen, and people to be loved. Relax, and watch life happen in the blooming of flowers, the rising of the sun, or the changing of the seasons. Get involved with life, and enjoy the journey.

Make a list of the great and

exciting things happening in your

life right now.

What are you willing

to do today to start enjoying

these things?

DAY
18

Honesty

You cannot fix what you will not face.

—JAMES BALDWIN,
author

AVE YOU EVER resisted saying what you were really feeling? Have you ever held back because you didn't want to hurt the other person's feelings?

No matter where we go or what we do, we have to be honest with ourselves and others; yet as men (and especially as humans!), being honest with others is one of the most difficult things to do. We become stressed, depressed, anxious, and uncomfortable when we are confronted with being honest and we try to avoid dealing with the situation or the person.

As men, we hold Spirit back because we think the other person may not like us, or we may hurt their feelings if we are honest. We don't take into consideration our own feelings. We suffer in silence and wish that we had said something.

If you have been placed in an uncomfortable situation, and someone wants to know how you feel about it, be honest. Tell him or her how you feel. When you are honest with someone you both should feel empowered. Being honest is not giving someone your opinion; rather, it is providing an outlet for you to discuss openly your feelings and emotions, making way for a "clearing." Everyone has an opinion; however, it is not your truth. Your truth is expressing from your feelings, your Spirit. It's not your opinion when you tell someone that what they said is damaging or hurtful. You are expressing from the truth of your emotions and how it has made you feel.

When you are honest with yourself, it allows Spirit to come through. You no longer feel compelled to hide behind facades or images. You can be who you are and feel comfortable with yourself.

In dealing directly with something, your honesty saves you and others time. When you are genuine, people will respect you for being open with your feelings. In turn, they will be authentic with you. When you are honest, Spirit opens up and the pureness of your being is able to be relaxed, loving, and free.

EXERCISE

Whom have you not been

honest with? In what

ways can you start being honest

with yourself and others?

Breathe

Then the Lord God formed man of dust from
the ground, and breathed into his nostrils the
breath of life; and man became a living being.

—GENESIS 2:7

T O LIVE IS to breathe. To have clarity is to breathe. Breathing is the most important aspect of living.

When we become frustrated, stressed, and upset, our breathing quickens. We become confused. Life is happening; it's coming too fast. Our families are demanding, our jobs want more time, we want to be on top, and our loved ones need us home. This is how our life appears. We become so bombarded with demands and pressures to be and do *more*.

When that happens, stop and breathe, just breathe.

When was the last time you sat down and took a deep breath? When was the last time you exhaled? You probably can't remember.

Next time you're in a situation in which things are happening fast, or when you become upset and frustrated, or you are in a situation in which you can't think, just breathe. Take some deep breaths and allow yourself to relax and become clear. Take in a deep breath and exhale. Release all the negative energy and toxins.

Today, breathe for Spirit. Spirit can work better when you are clear and relaxed.

EXERCISE

Practice breathing deeply.

Do you notice any changes

in your being? If so,

what have you noticed?

DAY
20

Treat Yourself

Ask, and it will be given you. . . .

— MATTHEW 7:7

HEN WAS THE last time you bought yourself a terrific meal? The last time you bought yourself a good book? The last time you went on an outing or trip? The last time you got a massage? The last time you got a manicure or pedicure? (Yes, men get manicures and pedicures.)

Sometimes in our lives we have to make sure everyone else is being taken care of, cater to others' needs, and we neglect our own. There is nothing wrong with helping others, but when was the last time you treated *yourself*?

You have to treat yourself as you treat others. If you are loving and caring for others, then treat yourself to some tender, loving care. We are deserving of all we give and expect; however, we don't expect it for ourselves.

Today, make plans to treat yourself. Decide you are going to take that trip you've been thinking about. Decide you are going to buy that suit you've been eyeing. Decide you are going to get that one-hour massage. Treat yourself to whatever it is you've been putting off, and really enjoy it.

Make a list of all the things

you can do to treat yourself.

How are you going to start

treating yourself to these things?

D A Y

21

Remember Your Past, So As Not to Repeat It

When the history books are written in future generations, the historians will have to pause and say, "There lived a great people—a black people—who injected new meaning and dignity into the veins of civilization."

— MARTIN LUTHER KING, JR.

OU'VE DONE OR tried something, and it didn't work. You've made that mistake before. You keep repeating the same mistakes but don't learn the lesson. We repeat our past because we fail to remember what happened. We fail to learn the many lessons that life so graciously provides us.

Sometimes we can be hardheaded: We don't pay attention. We insist on doing things our way. We are not clear and open to the fact that there is nothing new under the sun. There is nothing that has not been done already. We are doing nothing more than reinventing the wheel.

If we are to move forward in life, we have to pay attention to our past. Recognize what happened, study it, and find new sources of life experiences.

Remembering the past will allow new possibilities to present themselves and help Spirit assist you in your growth. Remember your past, but don't stay stuck there, reliving it.

Today, remember your past, so as not to repeat it. Know that life is constantly moving and that if you are stuck in the past, you will repeat it. So move progressively forward in the direction of life and be evermore present.

What situation in your past

are you ready to release, so

you can move on in your life?

And This, Too, Shall Pass

Grandma used to tell me, "Chile, you're like a biscuit in the oven, you're hot, but you're not done yet. Keep rising, my child, keep rising . . ."

— CHRISTOPHER MONTGOMERY,
corporate strategy consultant

ET'S FACE IT: To be in the middle of the storm and not know what is going to happen is not a good feeling. Chaos and mayhem are happening all around you. It's one thing after another, coming from your job, family, or friends. Life is not playing fair with you. Things are happening so fast that you just want to give up. You may lose your job, end a relationship you hoped would last forever, or fall victim to an unforeseen expense that depletes your bank account.

Hold on, because this, too, shall pass. Sometimes life has a funny way of happening to you when you least expect it. You are caught off guard, caught in the tailspin, barely hanging on.

Most times, life is just giving you a shake-up, trying to get your attention because you have not been paying attention. Life is waking you up. It may seem unfair that tragedy has to occur for you to wake up, that some unforeseen event calls for your attention. Know that this, too, shall pass.

You will have to rely on your faith, allow Spirit to guide you. Sit and be still. Let whatever it is take its course. Allow yourself to feel the emotions.

Breathe, and breathe some more.

Today, know that you are a magnificent being and that what you are encountering is an opportunity for you to wake up, be alive in the moment, and know that this, too, shall pass.

EXERCISE

What event in your life is

causing you to wake up?

DAY

Live

There will always be men struggling to change, and there will always be those who are controlled by the past.

—ERNEST J. GAINES,
author

WHEN ASKED HOW we are doing, our response may be "I'm surviving" or "I'm struggling, right now." Who are you struggling with? *What* are you struggling with? Can you literally struggle with your money or living situation? Do material things have you struggling to live?

As men, we have developed a survival technique, behaving as if everything we do is about surviving and fighting. We are fighting for our lives, fighting for our jobs, or fighting just to be fighting. We are surviving our money issues, we are surviving in our jobs, and we are surviving in our relationships.

Somewhere, someone told us that we had to fight for what we wanted, that what we get has to be worth fighting for. We are so caught up in the fight that we start only surviving. We are constantly treading water. We are not living.

When we think of ourselves as "surviving," that is how life will present itself to us. Struggling and surviving is not living. We miss out on life. We become bitter, angry, envious, and hurt. We feel that we have not been dealt a fair hand, that life is unfair.

Developing this attitude does not fully allow you to access life. How can you really live if you are only surviving? What you have is ample enough for you; yet as men, we feel we deserve more. Yes, you do deserve more; however, you have to enjoy what you have now so that you will be able to enjoy more of what you desire.

Today, start living and enjoying what you have. When you start to live, you fully access Spirit.

Make a list of all the things

you are struggling for.

What are you ready to start

living for?

D A Y

24

Honor Others

I am not ashamed of my grandparents for having been slaves. I am only ashamed of myself for having at one time been ashamed.

— RALPH ELLISON,
author

HERE ARE PEOPLE who have helped you along the way, people who have given you insight and provided some kind words or passed on their knowledge to you. There are those in our communities who have served as our surrogate family members. There are those who are constantly involved in the empowerment and preservation of our history.

We get so involved with our own lives and day-to-day schedules that we forget about the people involved in the bigger picture of how we shape our lives and communities. These people are making sure legislative bills that work for us are passed, our voices heard, and our images portrayed positively on screen. They are the silent warriors we fail to notice.

Honor others who have come before you, those who consistently show up for our communities and our lives—people involved in politics, education, economics, entertainment, as well as the health sector. Honor those who walked miles to work as a boycott. Honor those who sat in at the lunch counters and protested businesses that refused to serve people of color. Honor those who endured pain, hatred, and physical abuse far more than we can imagine. Honor your friends, family, and loved ones. Honor people who are important to you and help shape your life.

Today, write a thank-you letter to the congressperson of your state or send a memento to a family member who has been instrumental in your life. Acknowledge your pastor, police officer, or doctor. Honor others who take a stand for your life.

EXERCISE

Who will you honor and why?

D A Y

Honor Yourself

Take pride in how far you have come, have faith in how far you can go.

—ANONYMOUS

Y OU'VE DONE IT! You got the promotion or the raise. You made the career change. You helped your brother. You are a mentor. You are helping to shape the community in which you live. You are a good husband, father, brother, friend, and lover. Honor yourself.

You endured the situation or problem you were facing. You listened to Spirit and allowed it to guide you. You have made a difference not only with others, but within yourself. Honor yourself.

You were a silent warrior. You made an anonymous donation to a charity or friend. You got involved with your community. You made a phone call to save someone. You helped a co-worker or colleague. You voted. Honor yourself.

Take the time to acknowledge the work of Spirit in your life. Recognize the many times you listened to guidance and obeyed. Note the many times Spirit reminded you of how important your contribution to life is.

Honor yourself for your many accomplishments, which may seem to be small now. Acknowledge graduating from high school or college, getting your job promotion, or being nominated for an award. Celebrate your ability to move out on your own and get your first apartment or buy your first home. There are many things to honor, pay homage to, and be thankful to Spirit for. Always remember from whence all blessings come.

Honoring yourself opens the space for Spirit to be open in love, open in sharing, and open in happiness. You can smile within and know that you are being completely free with yourself. When you honor yourself, you give way to grace.

Today, honor yourself.

What are some of your

accomplishments? How will

you honor yourself?

Be an Inspiration

Today, I am going to be the best that I can be—
you never know whose life you could make a
difference in, being the best you can be.

— MECHEL THOMPSON,
restaurateur

EMEMBER WHEN OUR parents told us to do as they say and not as they do? Was it because they knew we would pick up their habits and behaviors? Is it because they knew that they had to be on their best behaviors around us?

Our children are watching us. Our friends are watching us. Our families are watching us. People we don't know are watching us. While they are watching us, let's be an inspiration.

To be an inspiration is to inspire others with your goodness and love. Give a kind word or commit an act of kindness, and your action will invoke within others the need to pass the inspiration along to someone else.

Sometimes the little gestures of saying hello to someone, giving up your seat to an elderly person or pregnant woman on the subway or bus, or even opening the door for an elderly person or woman are enough to inspire them to move beyond their circumstances. Going the extra mile and doing something thought to be impossible can inspire others. When people see someone close to them achieve something great, they then feel that they can achieve it for themselves.

Today, when you feel inspired to do something, do it. When you feel inspired to say something, say it. Allow your Spirit to express what you are experiencing. There is no random reason why you feel compelled to say something or do something to inspire someone. What you are feeling is a connection with them. Embrace it and you will feel complete. This is giving unto yourself in actuality.

EXERCISE

In what ways can you

be an inspiration?

DAY

27

Be Your Dream

Oprah Winfrey once said, "If we could only align ourselves with greatness, there's no limit to what we can be and accomplish." I have a sign above my desk in large capital letters: ALIGN YOURSELF WITH GREATNESS. I look at it every day, and it gives me strength.

— MARLYNN SNYDER,
entertainment public relations executive

VERYONE TELLS YOU to "follow your dream," but following means you are not actually *there*; you are chasing after something. It is there, it exists, and you can see it. You are getting closer and closer. Stop *following* your dream and *be* your dream.

In following your dream, you are actually saying that it exists outside of you, that it is somewhere out there. Within you, you already are your dream: the doctor, lawyer, actor, musician, producer, or artist. Be your dream.

You are what you desire. You are your dreams. They already exist in you. All you have to do is access your dreams, and life will help you sustain them.

Being your dream allows you to be fully expressed in Spirit. You can start being an artist, doctor, lawyer, or whatever your dream is. By making your dreams happen, you begin to experience what it is to be that which you are. For example, if your wish is to be your own boss and run your own company, proclaim to yourself, "I am the president of Me, Inc." Write down a concrete idea of your dream business and what it is about, including what services your business provides and who are the consumers buying your product. Tell everyone you meet about your business and watch as Spirit provides many opportunities for you to start living in your dream of being a business owner. You will start to notice business seminars being offered. You will begin to notice people talking about the service you are going to provide and how they have been looking for someone with that particular service. You will also begin to notice how many possibilities will begin to flow effortlessly toward you.

Today, start being your dream, and your dream will become a reality.

List all of your dreams.

How can you make your

dreams into reality?

DAY
28

Be Love

When you say "I love you," you are actually saying you have awakened a place in me where I am love.

—JOHN ROGERS,
author

OU CANNOT BE *in* love: Love is who you are. Love is what you are made from. Love is what you live.

To be love is to have no judgments. To be love is to have no hate, anger, bitterness, or envy. While these emotions are part of who we are as humans, we can choose how we respond or who we will be in any moment.

There are two places where emotions exist: You are either operating from fear or love. With fear comes hate, envy, bitterness, and anger. From love comes joy, happiness, creation, courage, and peace.

Operating from love is much easier than operating from fear. We most often choose to function from fear because it is familiar and we are not certain of the situation, or of the other person's intentions. But, if you choose love, you will not concern yourself with the outcome because you will be performing from love.

To be love is to love yourself, everything about yourself—your physical, emotional, and mental self. To be love is loving yourself when you think you have failed, loving yourself when you make a mistake, loving yourself even when you have not been obedient to Spirit. Be love.

Today, be love with yourself. Be love with your family. Allow them to be who they are. Love them as they are. Be love with your friends. Be love with your mate. Be love in all circumstances, and love will want to be with you.

In what ways can you

access love in your life?

Make a list of all the people

you can start loving

(and include yourself

at the top of the list!).

Be Present

You don't own the future, you don't own the past. Today is all you have.

— LES BROWN,
author, motivational speaker

YOUR LIFE IS happening *right now*. Every second of life, you are making a choice, whether you know it or not. You are choosing how you are going to live and be in life. Why not be present in life, too?

We are all involved in life. We are walking, talking, participating in life, and yet we are not conscious of the choices we are making. We become conscious only when something happens. Be present to life. Notice the decisions and choices you make. Become aware of what is happening around you. See the direction in which life is guiding you.

Being present requires that you be involved in life. You have to be consciously committed to take charge and have life move in the direction you want.

Being present is being fully there with your family, friends, and mate. Be with your family in conversation. Enjoy their presence. Be present to your friends. Acknowledge their existence and their purpose in your life. Be present to your mate. When you are in conversation, listen to your mate. Open yourself to their feelings and your own. When you are having dinner, be present. When you are making love, be present.

Today, allow yourself to be in the moment. Don't think or worry about tomorrow, the paper that's due, the e-mails you have to check, or the bills that need to be paid. Today is a gift, which is why it is called "the present."

How can you be present

in your life?

You Are Complete

Having begun with the Spirit, are you now ending with the flesh?

— GALATIANS 3:3

OU ARE DIVINELY created. You are from the essence of love. There are no flaws in love, thus you are complete the way you are.

We think we need more of this and more of that. We think having a car or a house, more clothes, a larger TV, bigger office space, louder speakers, or more money will make us whole. We think obtaining more material things will complete us. Material things are nice to have, but they won't complete us.

We even think that having someone special in our lives will make us complete. A mate or girlfriend can add to your life, but they will not make you complete. The other person will help you access something within yourself, assist you in feeling love when you feel you can't. They can help you access your joy when you feel you have no joy. The other person is not giving you these feelings, but only helping you access what is already within you.

We are made up of everything, every emotion and feeling. Love, anger, happiness, sadness, joy, bitterness, courage, and peace exist in us. Our Spirit is actually *engaging us to the feeling of the emotion,* so Spirit may have the experience we are having. Remember God's Spirit dwells within each and every one of us and the emotions we experience are reflected on our Spirit.

Today, know you are complete. Access your inner being so your life can be filled with what you desire. If you desire love, then be full of love. If you desire joy, then be joyous. If you desire happiness, then be happy. The possibility already exists within each and every one of us.

In what ways do

you feel incomplete?

What can you do to allow

yourself to feel complete?

RECOMMENDED
READING LIST

The Holy Bible

Brown, Les, *Live Your Dreams*, William Morrow & Co.

Chopra, Deepak, *The Seven Spiritual Laws of Success: A Practical Guide to the Fulfillment of Your Dreams*, Amber: Allen Publishing.

Coelho, Paulo, *The Alchemist: A Fable About Following Your Dream*, Harper San Francisco.

Dyer, Dr. Wayne W., *You'll See It When You Believe It: The Way to Your Personal Transformation*, HarperCollins Publishers.

Jakes, T. D., *Loose That Man and Let Him Go*, Bethany House Publishers.

Kimbro, Dennis Paul and Napoleon Hill, *Think and Grow Rich: A Black Choice*, Fawcett Book Group.

Scovel Shinn, Florence, *The Game of Life and How to Play It*, Simon & Schuster Trade Paperbacks.

Smiley, Tavis, *How to Make Black America Better: Leading African Americans Speak Out*, Alfred A. Knopf.

Vanzant, Iyanla, *Up from Here: Reclaiming the Male Spirit*, Harper San Francisco.

Walsch, Neale Donald, *Conversations with God: An Uncommon Dialogue, Books 1–3*, Hampton Roads Publishing Co., Inc.

Wilkinson, Bruce H., *The Prayer of Jabez: Breaking Through to the Blessed Life*, Multnomah Publishers, Inc.

Zukav, Gary, *The Seat of the Soul*, Simon & Schuster.

ACKNOWLEDGMENTS

To THE WORLD'S greatest editor, Melody Guy, and the Random House/Villard staff, thank you for believing in me and the book. You all have been such a great joy to work with. To my agent, Susan Raihofer, thanks for holding my hand during this process. You are simply amazing. To my confidante and angel, Dawn Marie Daniels, words simply cannot describe how much you mean to me. There are angels walking on earth and you are truly one of them.

I would like to thank my grandmother, Pearl Williams, for universal life and love. She taught me to be all that I could be in the world. To my aunt, Delisa Dean, thank you for understanding and giving me love. To my aunt, Priscilla Bradford, thank you for introducing me to God. You are a tremendous woman. Thank you to my best friend, Gordon Chambers, for your unending love to support all my efforts. My extraordinary spiritual life coach, Margaret Pazant, thank you for reintroducing me to myself. Thank you Louis Johnson, Jr., for your continuous support and encouragement. "And because God is the greatest power, we shall not be defeated." Thank you to Toni Blackman for the instinct to tell me it was time. Adeyemi Bandele, my spiritual mentor, I thank you for the guidance and direction. Your presence showed up as a father, and I thank you. To Dwayne Lucky for your unending support and friendship; Karu Daniels, you are a true friend indeed, and that's "for the record." The world's greatest publicist, Lea Byrd—you are so on point and dedicated, thank you. Gene Tolan for being an amazing support during my writing process. William Lyons III, thank you for your continuous generosity.

Thank you also to the men of Alpha Phi Alpha Fraternity, Inc., Steven and Keisha Combs Dent, Chris Beal, Ron Permel, Carmen Samuels Jackson, Mark Kornegay, Lydia Andrews and SIS Empowerment, Adolfo Vasquez, Tamara François, Sydney Margetson, Sharon Washington, Chrissy Murray, Kim Cooper, Tracy Hinds, the Harlem YMCA, MTV Networks, Inc., Erich Walker and ENYCE, Stacey Adams, Sandra Jackson and the Studio Museum in Harlem, Toni Brown, Mondella Jones, Max Rodriquez, Marcia Pendleton, Donna Walker Khune, Robin Green, Murphy Heyliger, Kevin McGruder, the Soul Food Program, Major Scurlock, Winsome Sinclair, Real Men Cook, Kevin Liles, Paul Butler, Tony Murphy, Jaleesa Hazzard, April Silver, Kevin Powell, Omar Tyree, E. Lynn Harris, Terri Woods, Kirk Burrows, Bill Brown, Lloyd Boston, Fred Jackson, Keelon Hawkins, Tarya Lewis, Phillip Ross, Max Siegel, Angelo Ellerbee, Terrie Williams, Iyanla Vanzant, Oprah Winfrey, Neale Donald Walsch, Les Brown, Gary Zukav, Dr. Phil McGraw, and Susan Taylor.

Thank you to all the men who dedicated the daily mantras that help get them through the day. Thank you all for your commitment to empowerment of our community. Tavis Smiley, thank you so much for your contribution to the book and the world. You are creating a dialogue much needed by the community. We honor you and thank you for being courageous and inspiring.

ABOUT THE AUTHOR

TERRANCE DEAN is the creator and founder of Men's Empowerment, Inc., an organization dedicated to empowering, encouraging, and enriching the lives of men of color in all aspects of their lives. He is also the creator of Education Source, which is an organization dedicated to educating community members by providing empowering seminars and workshops with leading professionals from the entertainment, hospitality, human resources, corporate, and political sectors. These seminars and workshops are designed to provide educational resources to individuals who are seeking knowledge, inspiration, and advancement in their careers, communities, and their individual lives.

Dean currently resides in Harlem in New York City, where he is working on a series of books geared to personal empowerment and spiritual development for men of color.

If you have enjoyed this book and would like to share your own personal experiences of encouragement or empowerment, please e-mail Terrance Dean at mensempowerment@aol.com.

Terrance Dean frequently speaks and lectures at various service and not-for-profit organizations. He is also a favorite at colleges and universities. If you are interested in booking him for your school or organization, you can contact him directly at mensempowerment@aol.com.

Printed in the United States
by Baker & Taylor Publisher Services